My Emotions
Emosyon Mwen Yo

CALM
KALM

A Crabtree Roots Book
Yon Liv Crabtree Rasin

AMY CULLIFORD
JEAN-PIERRE GASTON

Crabtree Publishing
crabtreebooks.com

School-to-Home Support for Caregivers and Teachers

This book helps children grow by letting them practice reading. Here are a few guiding questions to help the reader with building his or her comprehension skills. Possible answers appear here in red.

Before Reading:

- What do I think this book is about?
    - *This book is about how to feel calm.*
    - *This book is about what feeling calm looks or feels like.*
- What do I want to learn about this topic?
    - *I want to learn what makes people feel calm.*
    - *I want to learn what feeling calm looks like.*

During Reading:

- I wonder why...
    - *I wonder why we smile when we are calm.*
    - *I wonder why baths make people calm.*
- What have I learned so far?
    - *I have learned that drawing can make you feel calm.*
    - *I have learned that people sit when they are calm.*

After Reading:

- What details did I learn about this topic?
    - *I have learned that there are many ways you can feel calm.*
    - *I have learned that you can think things through when you are calm.*
- Read the book again and look for the vocabulary words.
    - *I see the word **drawing** on page 4 and the word **music** on page 8. The other vocabulary words are found on page 14.*

What makes you **calm**?

Kisa ki fè ou **kalm**?

Drawing makes me calm.

Desine fè mwem kalm.

I sit when I am calm.

Mwen chita lè mwen kalm.

Music makes me calm.

Mizik fè mwen kalm.

I can think when I am calm.

Mwen ka panse lè mwen kalm.

A **bath** makes me calm.

Benyen fè mwen kalm.

I **smile** when I am calm.

Mwen **souri** lè mwen kalm.

What makes you calm?

Kisa ki fè ou kalm?

Words to Know
Mo pouw Konnen

bath
benyen

calm
kalm

drawing
disene

music
mizik

smile
souri

40 Words

What makes you **calm**?

Drawing makes me calm.

I sit when I am calm.

Music makes me calm.

I can think when I am calm.

A **bath** makes me calm.

I **smile** when I am calm.

What makes you calm?

38mo

Kisa ki fè ou **kalm**?

Desine fè mwem kalm.

Mwen chita lè mwen kalm.

Mizik fè mwen kalm.

Mwen ka panse lè mwen kalm.

Benyen fè mwen kalm.

Mwen **souri** lè mwen kalm.

Kisa ki fè ou kalm?

My Emotions CALM

Emosyon Mwen Yo KALM

Crabtree Publishing

crabtreebooks.com 800-387-7650

Paperback 9781039624573
Ebook (pdf) 9781039625419
Epub 9781039624993

Printed in the U.S.A./CP102025

Library and Archives Canada Cataloguing in Publication
Available at the Library and Archives Canada

Library of Congress Cataloging-in-Publication Data
Available at the Library of Congress

Published in Canada
Crabtree Publishing
616 Welland Avenue
St. Catharines, Ontario
L2M 5V6

Published in the United States
Crabtree Publishing
347 Fifth Avenue
Suite 1402-145
New York, NY 10016

Written by: Amy Culliford
Designed by: Rhea Wallace
Series Development: James Earley
Proofreader: Ellen Rodger
Educational Consultant: Marie Lemke M.Ed.
Translator: Jean-Pierre Gaston
Production manager: Candice Campbell

Photographs: Shutterstock: Juan Pablo Gonzaález: cover; ZouZou: p. 1; ESB Professional: p. 3, 14; LightField Studio: p. 5, 14; Africa Studio: p. 8, 14; Newman Studio: p. 9, 14; Chz_mhOng: p. 10, 14; narikan: p. 11, 14; Rusian Shugushev: p. 13